Raising Money in Less Than 30 Days

A Guide for Individuals and Organizations

Susan Wright

A Citadel Press Book
Published by Carol Publishing Group

A Citadel Press Book
Published by Carol Publishing Group
Citadel Press is a registered trademark of Carol Communications, Inc.

Editorial Offices: 600 Madison Avenue, New York, N.Y. 10022
Sales and Distribution Offices: 120 Enterprise Avenue, Secaucus, N.J. 07094
In Canada: Canadian Manda Group, P.O. Box 920, Station U, Toronto, Ontario M8Z 5P9

Queries regarding rights and permissions should be addressed to Carol Publishing Group, 600 Madison Avenue, New York, N.Y. 10022

Carol Publishing Group books are available at special discounts for bulk purchases, for sales promotions, fund raising, or educational purposes. Special editions can be created to specifications. For details contact: Special Sales Department, Carol Publishing Group, 120 Enterprise Avenue, Secaucus, N.J. 07094

Manufactured in the United States of America

10 9 8 7 6 5 4 3 2 1

Library of Congress Cataloging-in-Publication Data

Wright, Susan (Susan G.)
   Raising money in less than 30 days / by Susan Wright.
      p.   cm.
   "A Learning Annex book."
   "A Citadel Press book."
   ISBN 0-8065-1460-4
   1. Fund raising.   I. Title.
HG177.W75   1993
658.15′224—dc20   93-11590
                                   CIP

Contents

PART THREE: *Grants*

Glossary of Terms

In order to make the most of this book, you should know a few key terms:

Capital   Money that is used for producing your service, product, or project.

Debt   Money that is owed with interest (a loan).

Equity   Partial ownership in a business that gives interest in the assets and earnings.

Grant   Money that is given to finance a particular project or business venture.

Stock   Partial ownership in a business which gives interest in the assets and the earnings, represented by a certificate.

Venture   A project, proposed business, or newer business.

Warrants   A guaranteed option of buying stock in a business at a future date for a specified price.

Introduction

Do you have an idea for a service or product but don't know how to raise the money you need to get a business started? Do you have a sole proprietorship you operate in your spare time that you would like to expand into a full-time career? Or do you already own a small business you want to make grow?

Then again, perhaps you have a project—a play you want to produce, a book you want to write, a seminar you want to give—but you don't know how to get enough money to actualize your dream.

Then this book is written for you. Look in the business section of any book store and you'll find scores of books on management, networking, and self-motivating techniques to help you succeed. There are also many books on sales techniques, hiring, organizing, even on how to read financial statements. But how do you go about getting money to begin the process?

You don't need rich relatives or a lot of collateral in order to get financing for your venture. There are literally billions of dollars available to individuals, entrepreneurs, and businesses in the form of grants, equity investments, and letters of credit. Even with the banking industry in a slump, there are a number of ways to get loans with extremely flexible terms—such as extended repayment periods, low interest rates, and cosigner guarantees.

The specific references in this book should help you find the right way to acquire funding for your venture. You'll find out about:

- different types of government assistance and how to apply
- foundation grants and proposal outlines
- private lending institutions
- venture capital and private funding
- creating a business plan to sell your idea or business
- public stock offerings for small businesses
- creative ways of raising money with your business such as direct mail, trade credit, or franchising

It's a fact that the more money you have to fund your venture, whether it's a start-up business or a special project, the more likely you are to succeed. The Census Bureau's 1992 survey of businesses showed that one-third of the general business population was seeded with less than $5,000, but half of the young companies on the *Inc. 500* companies started with at least $50,000.

So set your sights high and don't let the lack of start-up funds stop you from creating a successful venture.

Types of Financing

Like anything else, financing tends to build on itself. The more money you have, the more likely others will be to contribute capital to your venture.

Financing is usually defined in three stages:

Seed money (start-up funds)
Private financing (growth and expansion funds)
Public offering (for mature businesses)

You have many financing options. "Free money" from

foundation grants, straight debt (loan), or selling public or private equity in your business or venture (your profits pay the dividends). You may choose to finance your venture with a combination of financing—SBA loan and private debt, say, or a foundation grant and bank loan.

Foundation Grants

If your venture can qualify for a foundation or government grant, then by all means apply. This is a natural place to turn to if your venture is a onetime project, but don't neglect this rich source of funds if you are also planning on starting a new business. It doesn't matter if your venture is designed to be a profit maker. Certain areas of humanitarian interest— cultural or educational programs, health-related or social services—are often fully funded by private foundations or grants.

It makes sense to take this step first. A grant proposal is less involved than a professional "business plan" and can be considered the first step in the development of a business plan for next approaching private investors.

Loans

Loans are considered to be "straight debt" financing. Loans must be paid back, with interest, at specified times, and can be a drain on cash flow in a developing business. If you want to finance your venture with loans, then you'll need to decide on public or private debt, short- or long-term payment. Banks, insurance companies, and private individuals are sources of straight debt financing.

Most lending institutions want collateral or a cosigner (such as the Small Business Administration). They prefer easily liquidated assets, such as automobiles and houses. If you have an established business, many institutions prefer not to lend against inventory, but they will lend against bills, accounts, or notes that are due from others.

Selling Equity

When you sell equity, you are essentially selling stock in your venture, whether it is done privately or publicly. The investor receives payment on his investment, depending on the success of the venture and its growth.

There is a vast difference between selling equity publicly and selling it privately. The public sale of stock is regulated by the SEC and must be underwritten by an outside brokerage firm. This can't be done until your business is established and has books on which to base its financial stability.

The private equity investment is quite different. There are hundreds of firms whose sole business is to provide financing for new and growing businesses. Or you can approach individual investors, known as venture capitalists. Private investment can be used for seed money (start-up financing) as well as in raising capital for expansion. Most often, private investors fund ventures in a combination of ways—in the form of a loan as well as taking equity in your venture.

Part One
Loans

1 | *How to Get a Loan*

Most people who start a new business or invest in a project borrow at least part of the financing. If you have a good, profitable idea and plenty of ambition and drive, chances are you can make your initial loan pay off ten or more times over.

The first key to getting a loan, whether it's from a bank, a lending institution, or a friend or relative, is to be confident about your endeavor. How you enter the transaction will determine the results. Believe that you will get the loan, and most likely you will succeed.

Personal Loans

Contrary to what you might think, you don't have to have a business loan to start your business. Personal loans are the fastest, easiest loans to obtain.

Interest on a personal loan may be higher than on a business loan, but that little margin of difference won't really affect the profit-and-loss statement of a successful business. Besides, the interest is deductible on your income tax return.

One reason personal loans are so easy to get is because many loans don't require collateral. All it takes is your signature if you meet certain qualifying standards.

First, you must convince the lending institution that:

1. You will repay your loan on time.
2. You will use the money for something constructive.
3. This is just the beginning of your banking relationship.

Banks want to be sure that you are a steady, dependable person before they give you a loan. You'll have to prove this to them. Typical qualifying standards are the following:

1. You must have a steady job or income.
2. You've worked for one organization for at least six months.
3. You've lived at the same address for at least six months.
4. You have a telephone.
5. You have previous credit history or own a car or property.

Reasons for Wanting a Personal Loan
You may want a personal loan to start a business or venture, but, unfortunately, lending institutions won't give you a loan on a venture that hasn't been established yet. However, there are other reasons you can give for wanting a personal loan, including:

Auto or home repairs
Vacation
Educational expenses
Medical or dental work
Emergency expenses
Home improvement

Just because you receive a loan for this purpose doesn't mean the bank requires you to use it this way. The bank would rather you did something constructive with the loan than pay it off early after deciding you don't want to take the vacation you had planned.

In addition, you can apply for more than one loan from more than one banking institution. Unless you tell the banks, they won't know about it. Fill out the applications and apply for them all on the same day; that way you won't be lying about having other loans outstanding at the time of application.

Personal Credit

Many banks offer personal credit in the form of ready reserve, checking account backup, executive credit plans, etc. You can usually apply for these types of personal credit just on the basis of having maintained an account with your bank for a certain period of time.

Banks don't care why you've dipped into these funds as long as you pay the required amount each month. You can get thousands of dollars with just a signature if you have an established banking record.

Cosigners

Having a cosigner makes getting a loan much easier. Also, lending institutions don't examine your cosigner's earnings and dependability as carefully as they do yours. Just the fact that someone is willing to put his name and money on the line for you in case you can't make the payments is usually enough to convince loan officers that you're a good risk.

Your spouse isn't considered a cosigner. Most often, banks will ask that your spouse sign a personal loan as a matter of course. You'll have to turn to other members of your family or to your friends to find your cosigner.

Collateral

Collateral is any property or valuable asset which can be offered as security for a loan. If you are unable to repay your loan, the lender sells your collateral and receives the money in lieu of repayment. You receive any leftover money after payment of legal fees, fines, and interest.

Collateral can include:

Real estate
Home
Automobile(s)
Boat(s)
Jewelry
Stocks and bonds
Savings deposits
Insurance policy
Coins or stamps

Business collateral can include:

Business equipment
Real estate
Bills of lading
Warehouse receipts for goods in storage
Accounts and notes receivable
Contracts

Don't put up all your collateral for a single loan; conserve your collateral. And remember, once you pledge an item against a loan (i.e., use it as collateral) you can't use it on another loan application.

2 | *Business Loans*

To obtain a business loan, you usually have to have an operating business already established. Otherwise, you'll need a comprehensive business plan and a money manager who can speak the language of the lending officer.

Your business doesn't have to be profitable, only established. Pick a name for your business and join the appropriate organizations, such as The Federation of Independent Business, The American Management Association, The American Association of Professional Consultants, The American Women's Association, The American Women's Economic Development Corporation, The National Association for Female Executives. Designate an address (usually your home address) and phone number. Then print business cards and letterhead stationery. These are the basics in establishing a business.

Next, you need to understand how your business works. This is where a business plan or money manager comes in handy. Lending institutions like to know profit and loss, overhead, fixed expenses, etc. If you don't know that, maybe you need to find a business partner who can help you with the financial end of your venture.

The most important thing is to be prepared with the information that lenders are looking for. If you have your backup work done, then getting a loan won't be difficult.

Lenders will want to know:

1. What is the actual or potential profit of the venture?
2. What is the actual expense of the venture?
3. What is the ratio of fixed expenses (property, rent, equipment) to variable expenses (materials, production labor, etc.)?
4. How many people will be employed?
5. What will the borrowed money be used for?
6. What are the repayment terms you're seeking?

It's best to apply at banks and lending institutions where you already have established personal accounts. A bank likes repeat customers because it ensures the customer's dependability.

Types of business loans include:

1. Inventory loans
2. Working capital loans
3. Equipment loans
4. Property investment loans
5. Accounts receivable loans
6. Mortgage loans
7. Disaster loans

Short-Term Loans

Short-term loans may be the best way for you to get your financing. Short-term loans usually have repayment periods under a year—30, 60, 90, 120 days, etc.

You can always pay part of the loan back and renew the short-term loan for another 60 days. As long as you pay part of the loan, banks will usually agree to an extension if you pay the interest in advance.

Commercial Paper

If you own a business corporation, then commercial paper may be a good source of short-term money. Commercial paper is a promissory note sold by corporations to individuals or other corporations. These notes are unsecured—the corporation doesn't put up any collateral to guarantee payment.

You don't have to make monthly payments—the entire amount is due at the end of the loan period.

Compensating Balance Loans

If you have a business and money in an account, you can borrow against that money. Usually banks will lend you five times what you have in your account, as long as you sign a pledge not to touch the balance.

Compensating Balance Loans are made quickly—usually within 24 to 48 hours after you apply.

Revolving Credit

Revolving credit is a certain amount of money a bank sets aside as a credit to your business against which you can write checks. The only difference between revolving credit and a loan is that the money stays in the possession of the bank until you write the check.

There is usually a charge for setting up and maintaining your revolving credit, as well as interest on the money you've borrowed.

State and Local Loans

Many states, counties, and towns offer long-term, low-interest business loans to people who are starting a new business or expanding an established one that will bring jobs into the area. Typical areas of lending are:

Real estate financing
Construction financing
Business equipment financing

Contact your State Development Commission for more information on state and local loans. Once your state government has granted you a loan, it's easier to get local financing for your venture.

3 | *Private Lending Institutions*

Banking

Banks can both indirectly and directly help fund your venture and are the most common source of capital for inventories, short-term financing, etc.

However, during the 1980s, some 2,500 of the nation's 12,372 federally insured banks suffered financial difficulties or went out of business. This makes it harder for individuals or small businesses to obtain loans now. If you or your venture is turned down, it may be a reflection on the bank's assets—not your company's worth. You may have to try many different banks before you find one that is stable enough to have more lenient lending requirements.

Sometimes, a S.B.I.C. (small business investment company, funded by the government) will be associated with your bank, and if you go through that investment firm, it may be easier to receive equity financing for a start-up business.

Two-tier Lending

Since the country's current economic difficulties began in the late 1980s, a few commercial banks have begun offering small businesses a borrowing rate below the prime rate. A few percentage points can make all the difference in the world to a developing company.

For a list of banks that offer a two-tier lending rate, write to:

Chief Counsel for Advocacy
SBA
1441 L Street NW
Washington, D.C. 20005

Foreign-owned Banks

With the rapid expansion of foreign-owned banks in the United States, a rich source of funds has opened up for small companies. The U.S. dollar is continuing to be devalued, which makes investment in American businesses very lucrative for foreign institutions and individuals. Also, foreign-owned banks are not bound to obey U.S. banking regulations, which allows them a certain flexibility in terms.

Foreign-owned banks are usually located in metropolitan areas. Two of the large banks are Britain's Barclay Bank and the Bank of Montreal. You can consult your yellow pages for a foreign bank near you.

Finance Companies

These organizations often provide continuing financing to small businesses. Since they are more actively involved in your venture, they also tend to give advice on running the business as well. The cost may be higher than a simple bank loan, but the security of having additional capital if you need it may offset the difference.

Life Insurance Companies

Life insurance companies specialize in medium- to long-term credit and are state regulated as to the type of investments they are allowed to make. Many life insurance companies take stock warrants (options) in a company in exchange for capital as well as make loans

T.H.E. Insurance Company

T.H.E. Insurance Company issues an insurance policy to protect a lender against bankruptcy. With this insurance policy, private institutions are often more willing to finance your business.

T.H.E. appraises the collateral asset and insures to repossess it from the lender at the assessed rates. The value of a T.H.E. policy also allows more capital to be secured from lenders, because T.H.E. considers collateral that banks normally wouldn't, such as inventory.

You can write to T.H.E. Company for more information:

T.H.E. Company
180 Bent Street
Cambridge, MA 02141
(617) 494–5300

4 | *Federally Funded Loans*

Small Business Administration

There are two requirements to qualify for an SBA loan: you must have been turned down for a loan by a commercial lender and you must be able to collateralize the loan.

The interest rate of the loan hovers around 2.5 to 3 percent above the prime rate. Repayment terms vary from 7 to 25 years. SBA will restructure the loan if the growth of your business is slow, in order to try to guarantee repayment.

Most businesses are eligible for an SBA loan, except for projects dealing with real estate, publishing, or investment.

The SBA is discussed further in Chapter 5 (Small Business Administration Financing).

Farmers Home Loan

The Farmers Home Loan (FmHa) is the loan program of the Farmers Home Administration, offering guaranteed loans to growing businesses.

Unlike the SBA, an FmHa loan can be secured without proving that your company is unbankable. Also, the FmHa loan program doesn't have a $500,000 ceiling as the SBA programs have. In fact, FmHa loans have ranged from $7,000 to $33 million, with the average around $900,000.

Farmer Home Administration gives preference to distressed areas and rural communities of less than 25,000 inhabitants. It will loan money for any worthwhile business purpose. If your business creates jobs, then your loan has a greater chance of approval.

The minimum equity requirement up front is 10 percent, and the interest rate of the loans is about the same as it is with private lending institutions. The loans are fairly long term: 30 years for construction, 15 years for equipment, and 7 years for working capital.

There are over 1,800 county offices of the Farmers Home Administration, so there is probably one in your area. Or you can write to:

> Farmers Home Administration
> United States Department of Agriculture
> Washington, D.C. 20250

Economic Development Administration Funds

The federal government has designated two-thirds of all counties in the U.S. as "economically depressed." If your business is located in one of these counties, you may apply for a loan under the Economic Development Administration.

To qualify for a loan, your company must show that it has been unable to borrow from outside sources. Most of the loans are under $1 million.

The applicant must put up at least 15 percent of his own money and get 5 percent of the financing needed from his state or a nongovernmental community organization, such as Community Development Corporation.

For a list of economically depressed areas, application

forms, and other information, write to any of EDA's six regional offices; or:

> Office of Business Development
> Economic Development Administration
> Room 7876
> 14th/Constitution Avenue NW
> Washington, D.C. 20230
> (202) 377–2000

Other Federal Sources

Many other federal government agencies, departments, and administrations lend money to businesses, including:

Agency for International Development
Community Services Administration
Housing and Urban Development
Federal Reserve System
Health, Education, and Welfare Agency
Maritime Administration
Office of Trade Adjustment
Public Housing Administration
Treasury Department of the U.S.
Urban Renewal Administration

5 | *Small Business Administration Financing*

The Small Business Administration is an independent federal agency created by Congress in 1953 to assist, counsel, and protect American small businesses. The SBA provides financial assistance as well as management training.

In actuality, the Small Business Administration makes a limited number of loans to small businesses. More often, the SBA cosigns bank loans for small businesses after they are unable to obtain debt financing from banks on their own. As cosigner, the SBA agrees to pay between 50 percent and 90 percent of the loan in the event of a default.

Because the SBA caters to businesses that aren't bankable without its guarantee, they are dealing in medium-risk ventures. You or your company may lack capital or sufficient collateral or may have no track record in the field.

The SBA gives free management assistance to help ensure that its loans will be repaid. It also has relatively small loan awards, but over a longer term than is typical of bank loans.

Since the Small Business Administration is funded by Congress, it is a public service organization. It doesn't intend to make a profit from the loan it makes to you. The SBA sets limits on interest rates that banks can charge you on a loan it guarantees. Normally, this is several points below comparable bank loans.

17

Applications for SBA loan guarantees are first reviewed by your bank and then passed on to the SBA. You must include projections that indicate your company will be capable of repaying the loan. But even if you've been having a difficult time making ends meet in your business, the SBA will guarantee a loan if there are indications of improvement.

Gross Income Limit

Your company must meet the government's definition of a small business in order to apply for a loan. The SBA sets the standard-industrial-classification (SIC) code and adjusts the size limits for inflation or other changes. One standard is: no more than $2 million in net income; no more than $6 million in net worth.

Some industries have specific gross-income limits set out in the SIC code:

Industry	Gross-income limit
Advertising agencies	$5 million
Carpet-cleaning services	$5 million
Day-care services	$5 million
Computer repair	$18 million
Grocery store	$18 million

Reasons the SBA Will Reject You

There are certain types of ventures in which the SBA won't get involved, including:

1. Professional gambling
2. Businesses obtaining more than half their sales from alcoholic beverages
3. Newspapers, magazines, radio, or TV
4. Recreational facilities, unless they benefit the general public

5. Lending or investment firms (see *SBIC* at the end of this chapter)
6. Speculative real estate
7. Businesses that can get funds elsewhere

Loan Programs

The SBA has three programs through which direct loans or guaranteed bank loans are made. They are:

the-7A-term loan
the Economic Opportunity Loan (EOL)
the Operation Business Mainstream (OBM) loan

Direct loans (except in the EOL program) are currently granted for up to $100,000; but they are only available after the SBA's guarantee has been rejected by two banks and when the SBA has enough funds.

The 7A-Term-Loan Guarantee

The 7A-term-loan guarantee is made for up to $350,000 or 80 percent of the bank loan, whichever is less. The terms depend on what your business is planning to do with the loan. For working capital financing, the term of the loan is for up to 6 years. For purchasing fixed assets, the term is up to 10 years. For construction, the term is up to 15 years.

Fixed assets, real estate, or inventory are often used as security.

The Economic Opportunity Loan Program

The EOL program assists would-be business owners who can only contribute 20 percent of their capital needs. Since the EOL loans are limited to $50,000, your start-up costs would have to be under $60,000.

EOL loans are given to economically disadvantaged borrowers regardless of sex or race.

The Operation Business Mainstream Program

This program has the same terms as the 7A term loan, but it is intended to assist economically or socially disadvantaged minority group members (including women) to borrow up to 80 percent of their business needs.

Applicants must pledge all available collateral as security, but they can't be turned down for insufficient collateral.

Line-of-Credit Guarantees

The SBA also makes line-of-credit guarantees for up to $350,000. The line is secured by specific contracts for your business's product or service, and the funds may only be used to pay for materials and labor on the assigned contracts. Lines of credit typically run for a year.

SBA Nonbank Lenders

The financial decision for granting an SBA-guaranteed loan is made by banks or financial institutions, designated "certified lending institutions." You can cut the processing time if you obtain your loan through a certified lending institution.

Control Data Corporation is a financial institution authorized by the SBA to provide and prepare guaranteed loans. Control Data has business centers around the country offering data processing services, business planning, and marketing assistance. These business centers also offer a full range of lending services.

For more information, contact Control Data's Minneapolis office or a local Control Data business center.

Control Data Corporation
5241 Viking Drive
Bloomington, MN 55435
(612) 893–4200

The Money Store Investment Corporation offers SBA-guaranteed loans in branch locations in twelve states:

Money Store Investment Corporation
Springfield, N.J.
(201) 467–9000

Allied Lending Corporation provides SBA-guaranteed loans for the Washington, DC area:

Allied Lending Corporation
Washington, D.C.
(202) 331–1112

NIS Capital Funding Corporation provides SBA-guaranteed loans for New York State:

NIS Capital Funding Corporation
White Plains, N.Y.
(914) 428–8600

The First Commercial Credit Corporation provides SBA-guaranteed loans in Los Angeles:

The First Commercial Credit Corporation
Los Angeles, CA
(213) 937–0860

Small Business Investment Corporations

Small business investment corporations are licensed, regulated, and sometimes financed by the SBA. The SBICs supply venture capital and long-term financing to small businesses. There are about three hundred SBIC's in the country, and most are affiliated with an established financial institution, such as a bank.

Just as with any other venture capitalist firm, the task of the SBICs is to invest money in small business. The SBA financially assists SBICs in the form of favorable loans, so the SBICs in turn can support the growth and formation of small businesses.

There is a limit to what the SBIC can invest in a business—up to $100,000. There is also a great deal of paperwork necessary, since SBICs are funded by government money. For more information, call or write:

SBA (or SBIC Division)
1441 L Street NW
Washington, D.C. 20005

Another type of SBIC is the Minority Enterprise Small Business Investment Company (MESBIC), which provides financing and assistance to minority-owned businesses or economically disadvantaged persons. For more information, call or write:

American Association of MESBICs
1413 K Street, NW, 13th Floor
Washington, D.C. 20005
(202) 347–8600

Part Two
Selling Equity

6 | *Venture Capital*

The term "venture capital" refers to an investment of funds, usually in newer enterprises, businesses, or projects. The initial capital investment is also sometimes referred to as "seed money."

The initial stage of any business is the most exciting. If the business or project is financially successful, the investor who contributes in the beginning will gain the most. Many would-be entrepreneurs turn to their friends and relatives at this stage, but this can be disastrous. After all, you are looking for someone who can evaluate your business proposal as well as handle the money details of starting a new business. If you can't do that, then how do you expect your brother-in-law to be able to?

If you believe in your venture, then you have just as much a chance to convince a professional venture capitalist as your friends and relatives.

Private Financing

Private investment is any type of equity financing that is not made through a public (open to everyone) stock offering. It is not regulated by the SEC if fewer than 35 investors agree to hold stocks in your venture for more than two years. Often small, established businesses go this route because it saves the fees required to go public (brokerage houses, auditors, legal firms, and printers).

The main disadvantage of private financing is that shares are often sold at lower prices to investors than the price which the company could get from a public offering. This means that if you do eventually go public, the previous private financing will dilute the worth of your stock.

Venture Capitalists

There are about a thousand venture capital firms in the United States. More than half are also SBIC's, small business investment companies regulated by the federal Small Business Administration.

Different types of people invest in new businesses. Professionals, such as venture capitalists and "angels"; institutional investors; nonprofessional investors, such as doctors and lawyers; and friends and relatives. Nonprofessionals may invest with high expectations of quick profit. Many nonprofessional investors choose to provide advice as well.

Professional venture capitalists, on the other hand, make a business of investing in new ventures. They usually average one success in ten investments. When you approach an investor, he is determining not only if he will invest in your business but if you will be that rare "winner" he needs to stay in business himself.

Venture Capital Resource Publications

The Capital Publishing Company is the clearinghouse for most industry-wide information on venture capital. It offers several publications, including a monthly newsletter entitled *Venture Capital Journal.*

The ninth edition of the *Guide to Venture Capital Sources* is an informative guide that has articles by venture capitalists focusing on all phases of funding. Its most useful feature is a geographically-indexed directory with project, field, and geographical preferences included. For more information write or call:

Capital Publishing Corporation
2 Laurel Avenue
P.O. Box 348
Wellesley Hills, MA 02181
(617) 235–5405

The National Venture Capital Association offers its membership directory free on request:

National Venture Capital Association
1730 North Lynn Street
Suite 400
Arlington, VA 22209
(703) 528–4370

The National Association of Small Business Investment Companies (NASBIC) offers a twice-monthly newsletter from Washington, DC, which includes up-to-date information on the venture capital industry. The NASBIC membership directory can be purchased for $1 by writing to:

National Association of Small Business Investment
Companies
618 Washington Building
Washington, D.C. 20005
(202) 638–3411

A good reference for more than a thousand venture capital sources is *A Handbook of Business Finance and Capital Sources*. It contains information on financing techniques and instruments from both private and government sources of capital. Call or write:

Dileep Rao, Ph.D.
InterFinance Corporation
305 Foshay Tower
Minneapolis, MN 55402
(612) 338–8185

Corporate Venture Capital

There has recently been a resurgence in corporate venture capital. Essentially, this means that an established industrial firm invests in smaller businesses that help its own development.

The following firms have "development corporations" that are actively engaged in venture capital: Arthur D. Little, Bolt Beranek & Newman, Inc., Burroughs, Control Data, Corning, CTS, Dun & Bradstreet, Exxon, Fairchild Chamer, Gould, Inco, Innoven-Monsanto/Emerson, Johnson & Johnson, Motorola, National City Lines, NCR, Standard Oil of India, Syntex, Telescience, Textron, Time-Warner, TRW, Xerox.

The following firms are foreign-based companies that are also active in venture capital: Fujitsu, Jaeger, Lucas Industries, Mitsui, Nippon Electric, Northern Telecom, Robert Bosch, Seiko, Siemens, and VDO.

7 | *Selling Equity in Your Company*

As an entrepreneur, you are focused on the product or service you can provide. But if you want an investor to fund your venture, you have to address *his* concerns and needs in *his* language.

Key Components

A venture capitalist isn't an entrepreneur, like you. He evaluates the potential of businesses. Venture capitalists bet their money on you and your ability to stimulate the market and manage your proposed business. Your background, education, and experience are important criteria on which they base their investments. Certainly, your product and its market are important, but venture capitalists won't invest simply on the basis of a good marketing plan and a proven product. You have to sell yourself along with your proposed venture.

Management
Management is a key consideration for venture capitalists. They want to know the track record of founders and managers, including where they worked and how well they performed in the past. Their experience in marketing, finance, and production is extremely important. They are

also concerned with the credentials of the people managing the financial end—accountants and bankers.

Product
If there's something unique about your product or service, that is one hook for venture capitalists. Any patents you own, unusual technology, production methods, or increase in quality of a service or product will also help sell your proposal.

Return
Emphasize the growth potential of your business instead of confining your sales pitch to its more modest aims. Limited growth indicates there is small/slow return on investment.

Future Salability
Venture capitalists are also interested in the future salability of your company. The business of venture capitalists is to invest, become liquid, then invest again. Point out the larger publicly traded companies in the same industry. It will be easier for you to raise money if another company has already pioneered your product successfully.

Preselling

Consider the venture capitalist as a resource, just as your lawyers, consultants, and bankers are resources. Even if someone invests in your business proposal, that doesn't mean the investor controls the direction of your development. You are selling an investor a stake in the success of your business, a business you developed from your vision and through your own effort.

In order to sell from a position of strength, you must begin to sell before you *need* the money. For months in advance, tell potential investors about your exciting new company, through third parties or direct contact. Give them updates on developments as you bring together your business plan. When your plan is delivered, the investor already feels familiar with your company and is more receptive toward you.

Your attitude when talking with investors should be confident, as if you already have other investors interested. If you are extremely confident, you can discreetly imply that you may have to turn investors away. (This approach, if executed properly, is often successful.)

Delivering Your Business Plan

You may spend weeks or months in creating a business plan, but the way it arrives on an investor's desk will greatly determine its reception.

Using a form letter and sending out a blind mass mailing will get you very little attention, much less money. Theoretically, you could submit your plan to dozens of venture capitalists; but this may undermine your chances of raising funds rather than improve them. The SEC prefers for businesses not to send their business plans to more than 35 investors. Federal regulations limit you to a hundred potential investors, but state legislation could set the limit as low as 20 or 25, a number you must adhere to. You need to approach the people you want to have invest in your company selectively.

This doesn't mean you arrive with your business plan under your arm: It can be confusing and humbling to work your way through secretaries and assistants, trying to reach the investor.

The best way to deliver a plan is through a third party. The third party is, in effect, recommending you to the investor, prompting the investor to read the plan with more serious attention. You can use almost anyone whose liaison with the investor is positive: accountants, lawyers, consultants, bankers, or other entrepreneurs.

Getting a Commitment

Often, venture capitalists hesitate to be the first to invest in a new business. If you've shown an investor your business plan and he seems vaguely interested, then follow up with a meeting and proposition:

Say you want to raise $125,000. Tell the venture capitalist you have investors for the first $100,000 but that the last $25,000 is available. The investor doesn't have to sign anything now—all he has to do is give you his verbal commitment contingent on your getting the $100,000 first.

You can do this a few more times, gathering investors who are interested in your business. This will help you leverage the next investor into going first and actually making a commitment. Ask him for tentative percentages and terms, and continue negotiation even if you have to make concessions. That first investor is worth his weight in gold because the others will fall in line after him.

Terms of Investment

Most investors prefer to invest capital as part equity (stock) and part loan. The equity forms a funding foundation for the business, while the investor has the benefit of receiving payments with interest periodically.

Traditionally, venture capitalists will want a 50 percent to 60 percent share of your business outright when they invest capital. However, for start-up companies, a new idea is emerging—when the investor bets on your success. If your business succeeds (outdoing the projections of your business plan) then the investor accepts a smaller share of the company. If you don't do as well, the investor takes a larger share than he normally would have.

The following are terms that must be negotiated with your investors:

1. Seats on the board of directors, frequency of financial statements, and right of inspection of books.
2. Registration rights and timetables for selling the investor's stock or buying new stock first if the company goes public.
3. Working capital established, net worth of the company, and restrictions on dividends to keep the business from being drained of money.
4. Insurance issues settled: property and product liability insurance, and key-man life insurance.
5. Employment contracts with key personnel, specifying salary and bonus terms.

8 | *Creating a Business Plan*

$\mathbf{A}$ business plan is a document written to raise money for a company—whether to launch a new business or expand an existing small business. There are small differences between the two, mainly in the risk and reward factors. Business plans are used to raise private placement funds from venture capitalists.

If you want to start a business or expand the one you have, you need a business plan. Simply the act of putting the plan together forces you to assess your business and goals objectively. You can locate your strengths and weaknesses, spot problems before they overwhelm you, and plan a strategy to reach your goals. In addition, your business plan communicates your objectives to others.

If you create a business plan in a thorough, responsible manner, you will have a tool to help you manage your business better once you are funded. Since it's as much a learning experience as anything, it's better to create the business plan yourself rather than hire a professional to do it. It's easier to raise money if you understand every aspect of your business.

You can also save yourself the pain and frustration of opening a business that is doomed to failure. A well-researched business plan can tell you from the start if your venture is sound.

Describe your venture both clearly and completely. Don't

beat around the bush—sell your idea. Make the language optimistic, emphasizing the potential for growth in your particular field.

When venture capitalists read a business plan, they specifically look at:

1. The nature of the company and product
2. The terms of the investment deal
3. The latest balance sheet (established businesses)
4. The experience of management personnel
5. Anything that is unique about your product or proposal

Writing a Business Plan

Obviously, your pitch takes place in your business plan. The investor will try to topple your business assumptions, countering your upside projections with his opinion of downside risk. He will also consider your ability and background experience in order to determine if your projections can be realized.

An investor will skim—not read—your business plan and on the basis of that, most often will turn down your deal. Occasionally, an investor will confirm certain details of your plan and then reject the deal.

The two key components in presenting your business plan are clarity and brevity. Your company's name and location are of primary importance in compelling an investor to pick your plan from among the others on his desk and read it.

Don't bother submitting a partial business plan or a summary. It only delays the eventual reading of the entire business plan and can be frustrating to the investor. Make all the information available to your prospective investors, because if they want to know more, you don't serve your own needs by making them ask for it.

It's best if you can tailor the business plan to appeal to each potential investor. Venture capitalists have preferred areas of investment. You should emphasize aspects that are of particular interest to an investor, but don't ever exaggerate, lie, or inflate the sale projections.

Sample of a Business Plan

You can write a business plan without the assistance of a professional writing service, but it's likely you'll need some assistance from a lawyer to draw up the financial terms of the offering, as well as an accountant to make the projections. You can use the Pink Sheets (the over-the-counter market) to keep abreast of companies similar to your that are making public offerings, and use their projections as a basis for your own.

The purpose of a business plan is to raise capital from one or more private investors. You don't need to register your plan with the SEC since it is a private transaction.

Typically included in the plan are:

1. History of company or field
2. Business summary
3. Production and personnel plan
4. Products and services
5. Marketing and sales
6. Competition
7. Management
8. Financial reports
9. Enclosures

   I.   *History of Company or Field*
       Briefly summarize your proposed business
       endeavor, using examples of successful companies
       in your field.

II.   *Business Summary*
   A. Describe principal products or services,
      including brand names, price ranges, and
      quality.
   B. Describe the unique features of the business and
      products. Compare these objectively with the
      competition.
   C. Give specific goals on annual sales growth and
      profits, using as support material the financial
      statements of competition in your field.
   D. Describe patents or trademarks and other trade
      advantages, such as geographical location or
      labor incentives.
   E. Describe any trends in the business market or
      economy that may affect your company.

III.   *Production and Personnel Plan*
   A. Include description of production process.
   B. Name special skills needed in production.
   C. Specify the number of employees needed and
      their positions.
   D. Indicate the percentage of labor content in cost
      of goods.

IV.   *Products or Service*
   A. Name principal vendors and suppliers.
   B. Itemize materials and supplies, including
      storage requirements.
   C. List inventory.
   D. Identify distribution.

V.   *Marketing and Sales*
   A. Describe the market: history, size, trend, and
      your product's position in the market; identify
      established companies used as source material.
   B. Make forward and backward projections of the
      market—is it growing or stable or in decline?
   C. Identify your market (define your customers by
      age, sex, geography, minority group status or
      income).

      D. Describe how the product is sold.

      E. Define advertising: annual budget and media used.

VI. *Competition*

      A. List major competition, location, sales earnings, percent of market, and strengths and weaknesses.

      B. Indicate whether new competition is entering the field.

      C. Compare your prices and production with the competition.

      D. Determine your share of the market.

VII. *Management*

      A. Include resumes of management personnel.

      B. Prepare analysis of reputation, capabilities, and attitude.

      C. Include credit checks and personal financial statements of management personnel.

      D. List proposed salary and compensation for each member of management and/or owners, with salary increases.

VIII. *Financial Reports*

      A. Projected profit-and-loss statement (for 90 days and three years) includes:

        1. sales

        2. cost of goods

        3. overhead, fixed and variable

        4. selling expenses

        5. taxes

      B. Earnings projected (for one year).

      C. Accounting principles for depreciation, taxes, inventories, etc.

      D. Any lawsuits or bankruptcies.

      E. Principal bank.

      F. What you will use the investment for (working capital, equipment, land, etc.).

IX. *Enclosures*
 A. An important part of your business plan is the
 enclosures, which can catch an investor's eye
 and extend the consideration of your proposal.
 Enclosures include:
 1. product literature
 2. graphs
 3. unusual exhibits
 4. samples
 5. letters of recommendation
 6. letters of intent

Financial Terms

A complete business plan also includes the financial
terms of investment. Spell out the details plainly right in the
beginning of the plan so the investor can spend time on the
positive selling features instead of searching for what you
want from him.

It is very important, if you have an established business,
to have an audited financial statement from a reputable
accounting firm. A company-generated statement is not
given much credence since investors want outside con-
firmation that the information is accurate.

Aside from balance sheets, included in the financial
terms should be:

1. Percentage of company being sold
2. The total price for this percentage (per share
 figures can also be included)
3. The minimum investment or the number of
 investors sought
4. The value of the company
5. The terms of investment

Terms of Investment

Most venture capital firms prefer interest-bearing debt rather than a straight equity deal. It makes sense since the investor is assured of receiving an annual income on the investment. The following are specific terms:

1. **Common stock**   Or capital stock, when funds are initially put into a company. Stock is a certificate of ownership of equity in the company.
2. **Preferred stock**   It has advantages over common stock such as guaranteed dividends or prior rights in a liquidation.
3. **Debt with warrants**   A type of loan that obligates your company to repay a certain amount of money over a certain period of time at an agreed upon rate. The warrants are the right to buy shares of common stock at a fixed price sometime in the future.
4. **Convertible debentures**   A type of loan with the option of turning the remaining debt into stock.
5. **Debt**   A loan, either secured or unsecured. Secured debt is backed by an asset that is pledged to guarantee the payment of the debt. A house mortgage is a good example of secured debt. Any debt without an asset pledged as collateral is considered unsecured debt.

Sources of Information on Preparing a Business Plan

The *Small Business Reporter* has a series of guides, $2.00 each, on financing your company: "Financing a Small Business," "Steps to Starting a Business," and others. They also have specific guides for professionals starting a business, such as doctors, lawyers, etc.

Small Business Reporter
P.O. Box 37000
Bank of America
San Francisco, CA 94120
(415) 622–2491

Merrill Lynch has a free, 24-page book, *Understanding Financial Statements*. With this book, you'll learn how to read and understand a balance sheet, cash flow statement, and profit-and-loss statement. Any local Merrill Lynch office will send you a copy; or write to their general office:

Merrill Lynch Pierce Fenner & Smith Inc.
1 Liberty Plaza
New York, N.Y. 10007
(212) 637–7455
or:
Merrill Lynch
1185 Avenue of the Americas
New York, N.Y. 10016
(212) 328–8500

The Small Business Administration has several pamphlets on writing business plans. *Small Marketeer Aid #153: Business Plan for the Small Service Firm, Small Marketeer Aid #150: Business Plan for Retailer, Management Aid for Small Manufactures #218: Business Plan for Manufacturers.*

Small Business Administration (SBA)
P.O. Box 15434
Fort Worth, Texas 76119
(800) 368–5855

The Center for Entrepreneurial Management in New York also has books, audio tapes, guides, and workbooks that can help you write a business plan.

The Center for Entrepreneurial Management
180 Varick Street
New York, N.Y. 10014
(212) 633–0060

9 | *Public Stock Offerings*

A public stock offering provides equity capital, contributing working capital or allowing you to operate unprofitably while expanding your established business.

There is an unwritten rule on Wall Street defining a "good" company that's going public—one that has a million dollars in profits on ten million dollars in sales. If your business hasn't reached that stage, it's best to raise capital privately.

When you make a public stock offering, what you're doing is selling part of your business's equity, through an underwriter, to many small investors. An underwriter is a financial firm which "buys" a block of stock from you to sell to their customers.

One of the main tasks of your lawyer will be to negotiate the price per share. The underwriter will want the price low, while you will want it as high as possible without risking a downturn in price soon after the initial offering. Also key is the volume of shares to be traded in the over-the-counter (OTC) market. The initial price of the stock is entirely subjective and is determined by the underwriter.

Eligibility

Your company must meet certain qualifications before you can sell stock publicly. The New York Stock Exchange generally requires the following minimums for initial listing:

1. Demonstrated earning power under competitive conditions of $2.5 million before income taxes for the most recent year and $2 million pretax for each of the two preceding years.
2. Net tangible assets of 16 million.
3. A total of $16 million in market value of publicly held stock.
4. A total of one million common shares publicly held.
5. Two thousand holders of 100 shares or more of common stock.

In addition, other qualifications are considered, such as: the degree of national interest in the company; its relative position and stability in the industry; whether it is in an expanding industry with prospects of at least maintaining its relative position.

The Stock Market

Consider the condition of the stock market before making a public offering. The over-the-counter market, also known as the Pink Sheets, is where most small companies trade their stock. The number of initial public stock offerings can fluctuate from a few dozen to a few thousand businesses. Obviously, the way your stock sells depends on what else is being offered at the same time.

The Securities and Exchange Commission

Under the Securities Act of 1933, it is against the law to sell or promote stock before it is properly registered. If you are caught selling or promoting stock, you can destroy your offering and possibly your company.

Under the regulations of the Securities and Exchange Commission (SEC), all your financial information will be in the public domain.

Advantages of Public Offerings

What if your small business can barely meet the requirements of going public? Does that mean you should do it? Here's a list of a few of the advantages of going public.

1. **Additional Capital**   If your company needs money for long term expansion, then a public sale of equity may be the best answer. Short-term loans can strain cash flow. Equity is permanent capital, and in certain situations it may be cheaper than debt.
2. **Acquiring Loans**   Banks are more willing to lend to publicly held companies on favorable terms. This is because every aspect of your company is on public record, with daily updates in the form of over-the-counter quotes of stock prices.
3. **Repayment of Loans**   If your company is successful in going public and the after-market price of your stock is above the initial offering price, then your equity structure is considered sound. It is then easier to renegotiate loan repayments.

Disadvantages of Public Offerings

As a publicly held company, you have to adhere to specific regulations that ensure public security. Your own cooperation bylaws must be strictly followed, as well as SEC regulations. You have to consider your stockholders in every major decision, and this leads to bureaucratic red tape.

Since you have to please the stockholders, who will carefully follow the rise and fall of their dividends, you will be under pressure as to how to run your company. Inherently, you loose some, if not most, of your control over your company.

Employee Stock Option Trusts

If your business is publicly held, you may want to offer some of your equity to key employees by making the company's stock available to them at favorable prices. Employee stock option trusts (ESOPs) have positive tax benefits for both your business and the employee. They also increase the commitment of the employee in return for promise of capital gains.

Congress is currently legislating benefits to companies that adopt an ESOP, believing it will ease capital shortages. Already in place is the Tax Reduction Act of 1975, which gives an additional 1 percent investment tax credit to corporations with ESOPs.

ESOPs are used to raise money by getting employees to invest in the company. However, the ESOP also dilutes earnings per share and the owners' equity per share. ESOPs tend to benefit current shareholders by providing liquidity, while not offering much financing to the corporation itself.

Issuing stock to employees is a delicate matter which should be guided by a professional who is abreast of the regulations and benefits of ESOPs and profit sharing plans.

10 | *Underwriters*

The underwriter will select the best form of public offering depending on your financial needs and the condition of the stock market. Many underwriters specialize in certain business fields. It's best to find an underwriter in your area who is familiar with your type of business.

Underwiters are paid in many ways—in warrants and stock options for lower prices on stock in the future, as well as current discounts on share prices.

Although you shouldn't jump at the first offer you receive from an underwriter, the SEC doesn't like it when you try to create a bidding war over your offering. In fact, the SEC has rules regarding the number of investors you can show your deal to. Usually, good underwriters don't like it if you approach more than a dozen firms. Always submit your business plan to one underwriter at a time and wait for the reply before moving to your second choice.

There is a small group of financial consultants who make it their business to bring together underwriters and investment bankers with small growing businesses in need of money. These "finders" are usually paid on a percentage fee basis.

Underwriting Proposal

Like any business plan, your underwriting proposal is a selling tool. Emphasize the uniqueness of your company.

Among other things, your proposal should include complete information on the history of your company, your current financial statement, and the prospects of your company in its particular field.

The following is an outline of a typical underwriting proposal:

I. *The Company*
   A. Description of company
      1. Date and state of incorporation
      2. Principal stockholders
      3. Capital structure
      4. Location
II. *The Management*
   A. Resumes of key executives and officers of the company.
   B. Employment contracts with key executives
III. *The Product*
   A. Production
   B. Customer Profile
IV. *The Competition*
   A. Similar publicly held companies
   B. Growth potential of your company

Pricing Your Stock

The price of your stock is determined by the underwriter's evaluation of the company. The statistics of your company are compared with similar companies, particularly those that have already gone public. The underwriter tries to forecast the future earnings per share of your company.

The underwriter carefully considers what you intend to use the capital for—if it's in expansion, construction, and production improvement, that tends to indicate increased revenues. If it's just to increase working capital or pay old debt, the underwriter takes into account the fact that your company will remain at its current volume of sales.

Then there are the more subjective aspects of evaluating a company, such as: the competence of management running the company; the prestige of the company; equipment and facility condition; quality of product; and development plans.

11 | *Selling Your Company*

The alternative to selling equity in your company to the public is to sell your entire business. Usually, the purchaser is a larger, public company, so the end result is the same. Your company receives a fresh source of capital, and you as the owner get cash or stock in the purchasing company. The downside is that you lose at least partial control of your company and become an employee and/or consultant, or leave altogether.

Many small businesses are purchased "out of bankruptcy." This way, the new owner isn't burdened with old debt.

Another alternative is to sell the assets or products of the business. With publicly held companies, this option may make more sense for a new owner than buying worthless stock as well as the assets of the company. However, terms must be agreed upon by stockholders before sales of assets can take place.

If you want to sell your business, then use a broker. Brokers make it their business to bring buyers and sellers together at the most beneficial prices, earning a percentage of the deal. Brokers include: management consultants, venture capitalists, stock brokers, bankers, legal firms, insurance agents, advertising agents, etc. Consult your local business directory or telephone book.

Liquidation Value

This is the value that is assigned to a business being sold in order to satisfy creditors. Tangible assets, such as land, usually has a liquidation value close to market value. Inventories, on the other hand, are usually valued at about 20 percent of cost. Most assets sold in liquidation have reduced prices.

The liquidation value is the difference between the value of the assets and the debt of the company. This method is only used if a company is in serious financial difficulty or if it is heavy with assets.

Book Value

Book value is what is shown on the books as net worth. This is determined by subtracting the liabilities from your net worth of assets. Or you can add profits earned to the initial total capital investment in the company.

Market Value

This is the most common method of evaluating the financial worth of a small business. It can be more subjective than straight "book value" calculations. Market value is what a buyer is willing to pay you.

12 | *Raising Money Creatively*

There will always be ways of raising money unique to your project or company. Be creative. Don't always assume there's one way of doing things. Listed below are just a few alternative methods for raising cash.

Private Debt

Seed money almost always includes funds from an entrepreneur's own or his family' money. However, consider carefully before borrowing money from family members. More than likely the family relationship will last longer than your proposed business. Starting a new business is risky even if you know your product or service is a "sure winner."

Family Corporations

High-tax-bracket families often invest money in risky business ventures in order to write off their losses. Unless you happen to know a lot of rich, sympathetic people, brokers are the best sources for private investors of this sort.

Trade Credit

A good short-term source of funds is trade credit. This entails a delay between the delivery of goods and payment—

receiving inventory without immediately paying for it or receiving prepayments for undelivered goods.

Trade credit can be a revolving window of increased cash flow that can be used to generate more cash.

Franchising Rights

Selling franchises is theoretically an excellent way to raise capital while stimulating your business growth at the same time. However, the time and effort involved in franchising—producing a business plan, marketing, training, consultation, and quality control—make this a difficult undertaking.

Foreign Rights

Patents or brand names can be sold or licensed to companies in foreign countries as a way to raise capital. While this is more convenient than going through the process of opening your business in that particular country, you trade the profits of that market for a much smaller lump sum.

Barter

With loans and venture capital difficult to acquire, many companies are turning to the nonmonetary form of exchange—barter.

Barter has traditionally only been employed on local or regional levels. For example, if your company is a restaurant, you could trade your service (in the form of customer credit) to a professional cleaning company, wholesaler, florist, etc., rather than pay for these services.

Advanced Artificial Intelligence Systems enables companies, tens of thousands eventually, to barter services nationwide through their computer system. AAIS is a growing service that plans to expand as more companies come on line.

Companies can list their products and services available for barter, as well as the services or products they need. The computer system prints out potential supply-versus-demand transactions, which are then presented to the company for the final decision. AISS receives a percentage of the transaction, usually 10 percent.

13 | *Direct Mail*

Whether you use it to advertise or create interest in your business, or to actively sell or solicit donations for a project, direct mail is an immediate profit maker.

The established response rate of direct mail is 2 percent. That means you have to make enough money from those 2 percent of sales or donations to cover the cost of the mailing. Everything else is profit.

One good aspect of direct mailing is that it has an accumulative effect. Your first mailing sets up your recipients to be more receptive to your next mailing.

Who Responds to Direct Mail

One piece of mail is not going to convince anyone he needs or wants something if he doesn't already believe it. That's why only 2 percent usually respond. No matter how persuasive you are in your mailing, it's too easy for the reader to throw it aside as soon as she disagrees with what you say.

If you are trying to produce a play and are soliciting local residents for donations, only those who are receptive to the idea will even think of responding with money. And if you're selling a product or service, the 2 percent who become your customers probably already wanted your product before you came along to help them get it. Don't try to convince your recipients that getting a rug cleaned is what they want—tell them that's what they want and then sell them on the reasons why you are the best one for the job.

Designing Direct Mail

One sure way to learn direct mail is to "adapt" someone else's success. To do this, you have to examine successful mailings. If a company continues to send direct mail, you know it is successful. Put your name on the mailing list of companies that are similar to your in type of product, production, or service.

Once you get the mailings, examine every aspect. The most successful direct mail involves the reader. This can simply mean there's more than one part in the direct mail piece. It may mean large, colorful, foldout brochures. It can mean gripping copy in a letter or an unusual size of envelope.

Other important aspects are: the type of mailing list you chose; the time of month or year you mail; the wording of your copy and variation in it from mailing to mailing. Times change. People think and feel differently about the same things at different times in their lives. You have to try to figure out if your recipients have changed since the last mailing.

Creating an Effective Response Card

When you are seeking donations for a project, the most important part of your direct mailing, aside from the copy, is the response card. You need to make it as easy as possible for people to respond. Here are a few suggestions:

1. Make your response card a separate piece in the mailing. If it is part of a brochure, then make sure it is easy to find (on the back page or inside back cover).
2. Make the response card easy to read, printed in bold clear type.
3. Offer as many choices as you can to the donor. You will get more responses the more choices you offer—the terms of payment (long or short), method of payment (credit card, check, or membership credit), and how you pay (phone, FAX, or return mail).
4. Make the instructions simple—use check boxes— don't make customers fill in a lot of information. The more they have to think about it, the less likely they are to give.

The Importance of Appearance

Many direct mail experts feel the outside is the most important piece in a mailing. If your customer doesn't open the mailing, then you can't make a sale.

You can make your direct mail look like any of the four basic kinds of mail:

a) Personal letters
b) Bills
c) Magazines and newspapers
d) Junk mail

Obviously, people tend to throw away junk mail or give it only the most cursory examination. A standard number-ten white business envelope is a symbol of junk mail. It looks ordinary and uninteresting. A smaller or larger envelope is better than a number ten. If you do want to go with that size, then at least use another color, such as beige or ivory.

Other signs of junk mail are labels and "teaser copy" on the envelope.

Personal letters get the most serious attention—but hand-written, hand-stamped envelopes are very expensive and time consuming.

It is easiest and cheapest for your direct mail to look like a bill. You can use a window envelope, with the address computer-printed and metered postage for reduced rates. Most people will at least open the envelope, interested in finding out what's inside.

Also, if you're trying for the mailing to look like a bill, make sure the words "Address Correction Requested" are under the return address. This should be included as standard practice on all mailings because you don't ever want to lose a name or address on your list. Attrition will shrink your customer base faster than anything.

Return Postage

A self-addressed envelope with business reply postage may be worth it in the long run because it takes effort out of the customer's response. She can do it right where she is reading the mailing, without rooting out a stamp or filing out an envelope.

Successful Copy

Though copy is intended to sell your product, you'll do better if you focus on directing your customers to the response part and urging them to act. Assume your customer wants what you have to offer and sell him on the idea of picking up a pen and committing himself *right now*.

Deadlines work, but you have to judge your customers carefully. If your service involves a big expense or lengthy time investment, then give your customer a longer deadline.

If it is a donation oriented mailing, then you want to provoke an immediate response to get as many impulse contributors as possible.

Mailing Lists

You have to target your mailing to people who will be interested in your product. The best people for you to sell to are people who have bought your product or service already. Always put your customers on your mailing list.

You can also "rent" lists from companies which have similar customer demographics as your own company. Nonprofit organizations sometimes share their lists with other, similar projects or organizations.

There are dozens of resources you can use in buying mailing lists. One significant source is the Direct Mail Fundraiser's Association, "Direct Mail List Rate and Data" by Standard Rate and Data Service.

Part Three
Grants

14 | *Applying for Grants*

There are billions of dollars available to individuals, entrepreneurs, and businesses in the form of grants. All you have to do is take the time to write for guidelines, then formulate a grant proposal for your venture (a shortened form of the business plan that's used to get public and private investment).

Write to the federal agencies and private foundations listed in the next two chapters for their guidelines in order to find out if you or your business qualifies. Don't waste time applying for grants that don't pertain to your type of venture. Keep in mind that many foundations fund businesses according to geographical location, so investigate nonprofit and government sources that are in your state.

Apply for as many grants and awards as you qualify for—once you've gathered the support material for your proposal, all it takes is writing a new cover letter and filling out the grant application.

Your personal financial situation is not as important in obtaining grants as it is in getting loans or equity financing. Even if you have money in the bank and a substantial income, that won't stop government agencies or foundations from granting you a lucrative award. Many private foundations actually prefer to grant money to responsible individuals and will even contribute to successful businesses if they further the aims of the foundation.

Creating a Grant Proposal

Like any application, neatness counts. Take time to type (double spaced) your proposal, essays, support material, and statement of purpose. This extra clarity will reflect well on your venture.

Make a copy of each application before sending it in. You may need to refer to a specific part when you follow up.

I. *Title Page*
    Always include a title page, with your complete name, address, and telephone number; current date; the complete name of the foundation, address, phone number, and contact name; and the name of the grant you are applying for.

II. *Proposal*
    In your proposal, you should describe your project or business both clearly and completely. Don't beat around the bush—sell the foundation on your venture. Make the language optimistic, emphasizing the potential for growth in your particular field, and the way in which your venture will contribute to the foundation's goals. Make sure you specifically address:
    A. What you intend to accomplish if you are funded (exactly what the product, service, project, or activity is).
    B. Who will support your business or who will you serve? Specifically define your customers by age, sex, geography, minority group status, or income.
    C. What your production methods are (the practical considerations of achieving your goals).
    D. What you will specifically use the funding for (working capital, equipment, land, etc.).

III. *Attachments*
    Each foundation will require different support materials. However, the following is a typical list of information you'll need to have on hand:

A. *Individual*
 1. Degrees and awards
 2. Resume of professional experience
 3. Portfolio (artwork, project summaries, etc.)
B. *Start-up Business*
 1. Projected profit-and-loss statements (for 90 days and three years)
 2. Earnings projection (for one year)
 3. Resumes of management personnel
 4. Personal IRS returns (past three years)
 5. Any pending lawsuits or bankruptcies
C. *Established Business:*
 1. Balance sheets
 2. Accounts receivable
 3. Profit-and-loss statements (for 90 days and three years)
 4. Earnings projection (for one year)
 5. Business and personal IRS returns (past three years)
 6. Machinery or equipment owned (value)
 7. Any pending lawsuits or bankruptcies
D. *Nonprofit Organization or Project Sponsored by Nonprofit*
 1. Budgets (last year, current year, and projected)
 2. Past and present funding support (government, corporate, and foundation)
 3. A list of your board of directors
 4. A copy of the nonprofit organization's 501 (C)(3) IRS letter that documents tax-exempt status.

References

The references you choose to include in your grant proposal will be very important. You usually won't have the opportunity to represent yourself outside of the proposal; however, if a foundation contacts your references, they can take the opportunity to sell you. Make sure the individuals you list are interested in helping you and are comfortable with discussing your professional assets.

15 | *Free Money*

Although it sounds like a fantasy, "free money" to fund your venture can be had if you know where to look. The four most typical areas to find funding for your venture are: Foundation Program-related Investments, "Flow-through funding" from Nonprofit Organizations, Federal Research and Development Awards, and Federal Agency Funding.

Foundation Program–Related Investments

Foundations make program-related grants to businesses, organizations, and individual who further the charitable aims of the foundation. You may never have considered it before, but nonprofit organizations do invest in business even if it's run for profit.

If you have an idea for a business or personal project that can be termed "socially beneficial," then you may be able to obtain start-up capital from a nonprofit foundation. PRIs are an excellent source of capital for both start-up and established businesses, as well as individuals.

There may be foundations out there that will fund your business or project—but it's up to you to find them. More information as well as an extensive list of foundations, their focus, and award amounts is appended to Chapter 16, on Foundation Program–related Investments.

The following are general reference sources which contain information on thousands of more foundations:

The Foundation Center
The Foundation Center is an information clearing house that maintains national libraries in Chicago, New York City, and Washington, D.C., as well as regional libraries in almost every state.

The Foundation Directory
The *Foundation Directory* lists 2,800 foundations. The directory lists the foundation's name and address, purpose and activities, and the number and dollar amounts of grants awarded each year. You can find this directory in any Public Library.

The Foundation Grants Index
The *Foundation Grants Index* lists grants of more than $5,000 made by the 300 major foundations. It lists the names of the recipients, the purposes of the grants, and the dollar amounts awarded. This also can be found in any large library.

Catalog of Federal Domestic Assistance
The *Catalog of Federal Domestic Assistance and the Annual Register of Grant Support* lists programs, procedures for requesting applications, names of agency officials, and awards given each year.

Profit Working With Nonprofit

A special exemption is sometimes needed by government agencies to give a grant to a for-profit business. More often, grants are awarded to nonprofit organizations, such as colleges, community organizations, or clubs, for a project that you as an entrepreneur can be subcontracted on. It may be in your interest to find such a link through a nonprofit organization and spearhead the acquisition of funds by which you and your business will profit.

Another alternative is for an individual or business to use an established nonprofit corporation as a "flow-through" utilizing their tax-exempt status. It's best to locate a nonprofit organization whose purpose and activities are compatible with yours, then work directly with the executives of the organization in proving your venture serves their goal.

In "flow-through" financing, the money is paid directly to the nonprofit organization, which in turn pays you. The established nonprofit organization is usually given 3 to 7 percent of the funding raised as a flow-through fee. There is no upfront fee paid to the sponsor or parent nonprofit organization.

To find a nonprofit organization that would be willing to sponsor you, check the directory of local nonprofit organizations available in your community library. Local health and welfare planning groups, as well as the community, city, and state-run bureaus can point you to nonprofit organizations that would be interested in your service or product. In addition, don't neglect the nationwide nonprofit organizations which have outlets in your area, such as the United Way, Salvation Army, etc. A reference book that contains a list of national organizations is the *Encyclopedia of Associations*.

Research and Development Grants

The 1982 Small Business Innovation Research Act, *SBIR*, ensures that small businesses receive a percentage of research and development awards made by federal agencies. Each participating agency makes awards to small businesses on a competitive basis.

Each federal agency with an R&D budget of over $100

million must devote 1.25 percent of their research funds to establish small business innovation research programs within the agency.

The SBIR has provided nearly $450 million in grant money, with more than three thousand businesses funded. Nearly 40 percent of all awards from the NSF have been to firms with fewer than ten employees.

The SBIR program not only provides seed money (from $30,000 to $50,000), but it also grants almost half these businesses with a second funding ($200,000 to $500,000) within 12 months.

In addition, outside financial investors are more willing to invest in a company that is receiving SBIR funds.

Federal agencies participating include: Department of Energy, Environmental Protection Agency; Department of Health and Human Services; Department of Transportation; Department of Defense; Department of the Interior; Nuclear Regulatory Commission; NASA; Department of Agriculture. For more information, call or write to the following agencies for their guidelines:

Department of Agriculture
Ms. A. Holiday Schauer
Office of Grants and Program Systems
Department of Agriculture
1300 Rosslyn Commonwealth Building
Suite 103
Arlington, VA 22209
(703) 235–2628

Department of Defense
Mr. Horace Crouch
Director, Small Business and Economic Utilization
Office of Secretary of Defense
Room 2A340, Pentagon
Washington, D.C. 20301
(202) 697–9383

Department of Education
Dr. Edward Esty
SBIR Program Coordinator
Office of Educational Research and Improvement
Department of Education
Mail Stop 40
Washington, D.C. 20208

Department of Energy
Mr. Mark Kurzius
c/o SBIR Program Manager
US Department of Energy
Washington, D.C. 20545

Department of Health and Human Services
Mr. Richard Clinkscales
Director, Office of Small and Disadvantaged Business
Utilization
Department of Health and Human Services
200 Independence Avenue, SW
Room 513D
Washington, D.C. 20201

Department of Interior
Chief Scientist
Bureau of Mines
U.S. Department of the Interior
2401 E. Street, NW
Washington, D.C. 20241

Department of Transportation
Director, Transportation System Center
Department of Transportation
Kendall Square
Cambridge, MA 02142

Environmental Protection Agency
Office of Research Grants and Centers
(RD 675)
Office of Research and Development
Environmental Protection Agency
401 M Street, SW
Washington, D.C. 20460

National Aeronautics and Space Administration
SBIR Office
Code R
National Aeronautics and Space Administration
600 Independence Avenue, SW
Washington, D.C. 20546

National Science Foundation
SBIR Program Manager
National Science Foundation
1800 G Street, NW
Washington, D.C. 20550

Nuclear Regulatory Commission
Director, Administration and Resource Staff
Office of Nuclear Regulatory Research
Nuclear Regulation Commission
Washington, D.C. 20460

Federal Agency Funding

Federal agencies are created to help the American public, and many agencies offer financial assistance to individuals and businesses that are in need. Following are federal agencies that you can contact in order to receive their funding guidelines. Also listed are the venture qualifications and the average award amounts.

CONSTRUCTION

Associate Administrator for Maritime Aids
Maritime Administration
Department of Transportation
Washington, D.C. 20590
(202) 366–0364

Restrictions: Payments designed to encourage the construction, reconstruction, reconditioning, or acquisition of merchant vessels needed for development.

Award: direct payments (dollar amounts not available).

Urban Mass Transportation Administration
Department of Transportation
400 7th Street, SW
Washington, D.C. 20590

Restrictions: Finance acquisition, construction, reconstruction, and improvement of facilities and equipment for use by mass transportation services.

GENERAL BUSINESS

Office of Small and Disadvantage Business Utilization
General Services Administration
Washington, D.C. 20405
(202) 501–1021

Restrictions: Provides small and disadvantaged business firms with advice and counseling on taking advantage of government contracting opportunities. Procurement and surplus sales contracts are available, as are concession contracts and construction contracts.

HUMANITIES

Division of Research Programs
Centers for Advanced Study
Room 318
National Endowment for the Humanities
1100 Pennsylvania Avenue NW
Washington, D.C. 20506
(202) 786–0204

Restrictions: Support to independent research centers, libraries, museums, and fellowship stipends.

Award average: $75,000

MINORITIES

Office of Program Development, Room 5096
Minority Business Development Agency
Department of Commerce
14th Street and Constitution Avenue, NW
Washington, D.C. 20230
(202) 377–5770

Restrictions: Project grants for businesses willing to provide free management and technical assistance to economically and socially disadvantaged individuals who need help in starting and/or operating businesses.

Award average: $212,000.

Associate Administrator for Minority Small Business and Capital Ownership Development
409 3rd Street, SW
Washington, D.C. 20416
(202) 205–6423

Restrictions: Project grants to give technical and management assistance to individuals and to private organizations to help them succeed with existing or potential businesses that are disadvantaged (socially and economically) and that are located in areas of high unemployment.

Award average: $78,600.

PROCUREMENT ASSISTANCE

Associate Administrator for Procurement Assistance
Small Business Administration
409 3rd Street, SW
Washington, D.C. 20416
(202) 205–6460

Restrictions: Assistance to small businesses to help them obtain contracts and subcontracts for federal government supplies and services, as well as to help them obtain property sold by the federal government.

PUBLISHING

Division of Research Programs, Texts/Publication
Room 318
National Endowment for the Humanities
1100 Pennsylvania Avenue, NW
Washington, D.C. 20506
(202) 786–0207

Restrictions: Project grants to publishing entities for the dissemination of works of scholarly distinction that, without support, could not be published.

Award average: $7,000

PHYSICAL DISASTER LOANS

Office of Disaster Assistance
Small Business Administration
409 3rd Street, SW
Washington, D.C. 20416
(202) 205–6734

Restrictions: Direct loans to victims (homeowners, renters, and businesses) of designated physical disasters for uninsured losses.

Loans: direct loans of up to $500,000 with interest not to exceed 8 percent.

REHABILITATION LOANS

Community Planning and Development
Office of Urban Rehabilitation
Department of Housing and Urban Development
451 7th Street, SW
Washington, D.C. 20410
(202) 708–1367

Restrictions: Direct loans to finance the rehabilitation of property in designated areas; funds may be used for residential, nonresidential, and mixed-use properties.

VETERANS

Loan Policy and Procedures Branch
Small Business Administration
409 3rd Street, SW
Washington, D.C. 20416
(202) 205–6570

Restrictions: Direct loans to small businesses owned by Vietnam–era and disabled veterans; funds may be used for construction, expansion, or conversion of facilities,

purchase of equipment, materials, or for working capital.
Loans: $1,000-$150,000.

WOMEN

Small Business Administration
Office of Women's Business Ownership
409 3rd Street, SW
Washington, D.C. 20416
(202) 205–6673

Restrictions: Grants for demonstration projects to benefit
small businesses owned and controlled by women;
demonstration projects will provide financial,
management, and marketing training and counseling
services to both start-up and established women's
businesses.

Award range: $35,000-$1 million.

16 | *Foundation Program–Related Investments Source Guide*

If you can think of a way your project or business benefits society, you can probably find a foundation that would help you get started. This includes businesses with such diverse focuses as: housing, medical research, environment, conservation, historic preservation, culture, civic programs, the arts, and health-related services.

In fact, foundations often invest in projects that many traditional investors would consider to be too risky or where the financial return may be low.

An art gallery or theater could be considered "cultural development." An adult education organization, a day-care center, or driving school could be considered "educational." A gardening firm or construction company could be involved in projects considered "community development." Or your construction company can get involved in historic preservation or building a park.

A magazine or newsletter about local areas or interests could be considered a "publication." Under "natural resource management," your boat rental company, fishing store, or ski shop could qualify. As for funding for "community and social services"—your restaurant could be involved in a "meals-on-wheels" program or you could supply a local homeless shelter with food or clothing from part of your inventory.

If you're an artist, a local foundation could commission your work to be displayed in a public area. Or your play could be funded and performed as a community service.

Even if your project or company doesn't fit one of these categories, you may be eligible by emphasizing an educational aspect to your service—offering seminars or workshops from your craft store or consulting firm, for example. There are dozens of foundations that support educational programs.

Foundation funding is too lucrative to ignore. The amount of awards can run from $5,000 to $100,000 or more.

Foundations

The following list gives the names, addresses, focus, and average award of foundations that grant program-related investments. The first group of foundations grant money nationwide, to humanitarian-oriented programs, projects, and businesses. These ventures could be culturally-related, civic, or social services, health or environmental businesses.

The second list is of foundations that grant money to one specific area of interest, such as the arts, environment, or education.

The third group of foundations is listed according to state. These foundations grant money only to businesses and individuals who are located in their state and serve the needs of the local residents.

NATIONAL FOUNDATIONS

Allstate Foundation
Allstate Plaza North
Northbrook, IL 60062
(708) 402–5502

Focus: self-help, self-motivation, education, civic affairs, health.

Award range: $5,000-$25,000

Annenberg Foundation
St. Davids Center
150 Radnor-Chester Road, Suite A-200
St. Davis, PA 19087

Focus: education, health, and cultural programs.

Award range: $25,000-$250,000

Carnegie Corporation of New York
437 Madison Avenue
New York, NY 10022
(212) 371–3200

Focus: education, human resource strength in developing countries.

Award range: $25,000-$300,000

The Ford Foundation
320 E. 43rd St.
New York, NY 10017
(212) 573–5000

Focus: urban development, social justice, education, culture, international affairs, population programs.

Award range: $25,000-$1.5 million

Hitachi Foundation
1509 22nd Street, NW
Washington, D.C. 20037
(202) 457–0588

Focus: arts, community/economic development, education, and technology.

Award average: $28,000.

The Joyce Foundation
135 South LaSale Street, Suite 4010
Chicago, IL 60603
(312) 782–2464

Focus: culture, conservation, education, economic development.

Award range: $5,000-$50,000.

Peter Kiewit Foundation
Woodmen Tower, Suite 900
17th and Farnam Streets
Omaha, NE 68102
(402) 344–7890

Focus: cultural programs, community development, education, social services.

Award range: $10,000-$100,000.

David H. Koch Charitable Trust
4111 E. 37th Street, N
Wichita, KS 67220
(316) 832–5227

Focus: arts, education, and public interest.

Award range: $10,000-$100,000.

Metropolitan Life Foundation
One Madison Avenue
New York, NY 10010
(212) 578–6272

Focus: education, health, social services, cultural programs.

Award range: $1,000-$25,000.

Charles Stewart Mott Foundation
1200 Mott Foundation Building
Flint, MI 48502
(313) 238–5651

Focus: community improvement and education.

Award range: $10,000-$100,000.

Northwest Area Foundation
E-1201 First National Bank Building
332 Minnesota St.
St. Paul, MN 55101
(612) 224–9635

Focus: economic development, natural resource management, and the arts.

Award range: $30,000-$300,000.

The Pew Charitable Trusts
Three Parkway, Suite 501
Philadelphia, PA 19102
(215) 568–3330

Focus: culture, education, religion, health, and human services.

Award range: $50,000-$200,000.

The Carl and Lily Pforzheimer Foundation
650 Madison Avenue, 23rd Floor
New York, NY 10022
(212) 223–6500

Focus: education, cultural programs, and health.

Award range: $10,000-$50,000.

Reader's Digest Foundation
Roaring Brook Road
Pleasantville, NY 10570
(914) 241–5370

Focus: social services, cultural programs, education.

Award range: $10,000-$60,000.

Rockefeller Foundation
1133 Avenue of the Americas
New York, NY 10036
(212) 869–8500

Focus: science, agriculture, health, arts, and humanities.

Award range: $10,000-$150,000.

The South Atlantic Foundation, Inc.
428 Bull Street
Savannah, GA 31401
(912) 238–3288

Focus: social services, health, education, and cultural programs.

Award range: $1,000-$20,000.

The Sonat Foundation, Inc.
1900 Fifth Avenue, N
P.O. Box 2563
Birmingham, AL 35202
(205) 325–7460

Focus: Education, social service, health agencies, community development, environmental concerns, and cultural programs.

Union Pacific Foundation
Martin Tower
Eighth and Eaton Avenue
Bethlehem, PA 18018
(215) 861–3225

Focus: education, health, culture, social services.

Award range: $1,000-$10,000.

Xerox Foundation
P.O. Box 1600
Stamford, CT 06904
(203) 968–3306

Focus: social, cultural, educational services.

SPECIFIC-FOCUS FOUNDATIONS

ARTS

GTE Foundation
One Stamford Forum
Stamford, CT 06904
(203) 965–3620

Focus: performing arts, educational programs.

Award range: Flexible.

Abe and Frances Lastfogel Foundation
c/o Wallin, Simon, Black, and Co.
1350 Avenue of the Americas
New York, NY 10019
(212) 586–5100

Focus: cultural programs and motion picture industry.

Award range: $120-$50,000.

CHRISTIAN

The Christian Workers Foundation
P.O. Box 457
Wolfeboro, NH 03896

Focus: evangelistic Christian organizations involved in youth work.

Layne Foundation
29214 Whites Point Drive
Rancho Palos Verdes, CA 90274
(213) 544–4700

Focus: Christian religious organizations.

Ida S. Miles Foundation
c/o Herbert A. Crew, Jr.
P.O. Box 853
Pacific Palisades, CA 90272
(213) 454–0448

Focus: world hunger, Christian mission education.

Raskob Foundation for Catholic Activities, Inc.
P.O. Box 4019
Wilmington, DE 19807
(302) 655–4440
Focus: Roman Catholic Church projects.

EDUCATION

American Honda Foundation
P.O. Box 2205
Torrance, CA 90509-2205
(213) 781–4090

Focus: Organizations supporting youth and scientific education.

BellSouth Foundation
c/o BellSouth Corporation
1155 Peachtree Street, NE, Room 7H08
Atlanta, GA 30367
(404) 249–2414

Focus: educational programs and telecommunications.

Award range: $6,000-$30,000.

The Coca-Cola Foundation
One Coca-Cola Plaza, NW
Atlanta, GA 30313
(404) 676–2680

Focus: education.

Award range: $10,000-$100,000.

Phil Hardin Foundation
c/o Citizens National Bank
P.O. Box 911
Meridian, MI 39302

Focus: education.

Award range: $1,000-$69,000.

The Powell Family Foundation
10990 Roe Avenue
P.O. Box 7270
Shawnee Mission, KS 66207
(913) 345–3000
Focus: education and youth agencies.
Award range: $1,000-$50,000.

Samuel B. Mosher Foundation
3278 Loma Riviera Drive
San Diego, CA 92110
(619) 226–6122
Focus: educational programs, cultural and youth-oriented organizations.

Smart Family Foundation
15 Benders Drive
Greenwich, CT 06831
(203) 531–1474
Focus: education organizations for children.

ENVIRONMENT

Island Foundation, Inc.
589 Mill St.
Marion, MA 02738
(508) 748–2809
Focus: environmental education and conservation.
Award range: $3,000-$20,000.

The McIntosh Foundation
215 5th St., Suite 100
West Palm Beach, FL 33401
(407) 832–8845
Focus: to support environmental lawsuits.
Award range: $400-$278,300.

HEALTH

The Robert Wood Johnson Foundation
P.O. Box 2316
Princeton, NJ 08543
(609) 452–8701
Focus: health-related programs.
Award range: $55,000-$200,000.

STATE

ARIZONA

Arizona Community Foundation
4350 E. Camelback Road, Suite 216C
Phoenix, AZ 85018
(602) 952–9954
Focus: Arizona–health programs, human services, conservation, community development.
Average award: $1000–$10,000

ARKANSAS

The Winthrop Rockefeller Foundation
308 E. 8th Street
Little Rock, AR 72220
Focus: Arkansas—local economic development.
Average award: $1,000–$5,000.

CALIFORNIA

California Community Foundation
606 South Olive Street, Suite 2400
Los Angeles, CA 90014
(213) 413–4042
Focus: California—Community development, human services, health, education, and culture.
Average award: $5,000–$25,000.

Community Foundation for Monterey County
P.O. Box 1384
Monterey, CA 93942
Focus: Social services, historic preservation, environment, health education, and the arts.
Average award: $500–$200,000

Corcoran Community Foundation
P.O. Box 457
Corcoran, CA 93212
(209) 992–5551
Focus: Corcoran, CA area—seed money, emergency funds, building funds, land acquisition, special projects, publications, conferences, and seminars.
Average award: $5,000

Wallace Alexander Gerbode Foundation
470 Columbus Avenue, Suite 209
San Francisco, CA 94133
(415) 391–0911
Focus: San Francisco Bay Area—innovative programs and projects with a direct impact on the residents.
Award range: $5,000–$25,000

The Luke B. Hancock Foundation
360 Bryant Street
Palo Alto, CA 94301
(415) 321–5536
Focus: San Francisco Bay Area—youth training and employment.
Award range: $1,000–$30,000

The James Irvine Foundation
One Market Plaza
Spear Tower, Suite 1715
San Francisco, CA 94105
(415) 777–2244

Focus: California—community development, culture, health, education and social concerns.

Award range: $25,000–$150,000

Marin Community Foundation
1100 Larkspur Landing Circle, Suite 365
Larkspur, CA 94939
(415) 461–3333

Focus: Marin County, CA—arts and humanities, education, environment, housing and community development, human needs, religion.

David and Lucile Packard Foundation
300 Second Street, Suite 200
Los Altos, CA 94022
(415) 948–7658

Focus: San Francisco Bay and Monterey Bay areas— educational, cultural, community development for population studies, film preservation, and studies of antiquity.

Award range: $5,000–$100,000

The Parker Foundation
1200 Prospect Street, Suite 575
La Jolla, CA 92037
(619) 456–3038

Focus: San Diego County—cultural and health-related programs.

Award range: $5,000–$15,000

The San Francisco Foundation
685 Market Street, Suite 910
San Francisco, CA 94105
(415) 495–3100

Focus: Bay Area—arts, health, education, environment.

Award range: $5,000–$50,000

The Times Mirror Foundation
Times Mirror Square
Los Angeles, CA 90053
(213) 237–3945

Focus: Southern California—education, community service, and culture.

Award range: $5,000–$200,000

COLORADO

Coors (Adolph) Foundation
350-C Clayton Street
Denver, CO 80206
(303) 388–1638

Focus: Colorado—building funds, social services and civic affairs.

Award range: $5,000–$20,000

Fishback Foundation Trust
Eight Village Rd.
Englewood, CO 90110
(303) 789–1753

Focus: Denver—health, education and culture.

Award range: $250–$10,000

Gates Foundation
3200 Cherry Creek South Drive, Suite 630
Denver, CO 80209
(303) 722–1881

Focus: Colorado—education and youth services, publications.

Award range: $5,000–$25,000

The Piton Foundation
Kittredge Building, Suite 700
511 16th Street
Denver, CO 90802
(303) 825–6246

Focus: Colorado—self-help organizations, education, housing.

Award range: $500–$30,000

CONNECTICUT

The Barnes Foundation, Inc.
P.O. Box 1560
Bristol, CT 06011
(203) 583–7070

Focus: educational programs.

Award range: $5,000–$10,000

DELAWARE

Crystall Trust
1088 DuPont Building
Wilmington, DE 19898

Focus: higher education and social/family services as well as cultural programs.

Award range: $10,000–$100,000

FLORIDA

Edyth Bush Charitable Foundation, Inc.
199 E. Welbourne Ave.
P.O. Box 1967
Winter Park, FL 32790
(407) 647–4322

Focus: human services, health, elderly, and youth.

Average award: $20,000–$75,000.

The Wilder Foundation
P.O. Box 99
Key Biscayne, FL 33149

Focus: cultural and educational funding.

Award range: $25–$87,000.

ILLINOIS

The Chicago Community Trust
222 North LaSalle Street, Suite 1400
Chicago, IL 60601
(312) 372–3356
Focus: health, social services, education, community service.
Award range: $10,000–$50,000.

The Field Foundation of Illinois, Inc.
135 South LaSale Street, Suite 1250
Chicago, IL 60603
(312) 263–3211
Focus: health, education, cultural activities.
Award range: $10,000–$20,000.

The Robert R. McCormick Tribune Foundation
435 North Michigan Avenue, Suite 770
Chicago, IL 60611
(312) 222–3510
Focus: education, health, cultural programs, conservation.
Award range: $2,500–$100,000.

INDIANA

The Indianapolis Foundation
615 N. Alabama Street, Room 119
Indianapolis, IN 46204
(317) 634–7497
Focus: community planning, education, health, family, and cultural programs.
Award range: $4,000–$50,000.

KENTUCKY

Bank of Louisville Charities, Inc.
500 W. Broadway
Louisville, KY 40202

Focus: cultural programs, education, and community development.

Award range: $25–$45,300.

Citizens Fidelity Foundation, Inc.
P.O. Box 33000
Louisville, KY 40232
(502) 581–2016

Focus: social services, cultural programs, and education.

LOUISIANA

The Lupin Foundation
3715 Prytania Street, Suite 307
New Orleans, LA 70115
(504) 897–6125

Focus: educations, arts, community development.

Award range: $170–$60,000.

MARYLAND

The Thomas B. and Elizabeth Sheridan Foundation
Executive Plaza II, Suite 604
11350 McCormick Road
Hunt Valley, MD 21031
(301) 771–0475

Focus: cultural and educational programs.

Award range: $500–$50,000.

MASSACHUSETTS

The Theodore Edson Parker Foundation
c/o Grants Management Associates, Inc.
230 Congress Street, 3rd Floor
Boston, MA 02110
(617) 426–7172

Focus: community development, arts, housing, social services, and minority concerns.

Award average: $30,000.

State Street Foundation
c/o State Street Bank and Trust Co.
P.O. Box 351
Boston, MA 02101
(617) 654–3381

Focus: cultural programs, education, health and human services.

Award range: $2,000–$103,000.

The Nathaniel and Elizabeth Stevens Foundation
P.O. Box 111
North Andover, MA 01845
(508) 688–7211

Focus: conservation, historic preservation, arts.

Award range: $2,000–$10,000.

MICHIGAN

Hudson-Webber Foundation
333 West Fort St., Suite 1310
Detroit, MI 48226
(313) 963–7777

Focus: art and cultural development, community development.

Award range: $20,000–$50,000.

MINNESOTA

Dellwood Foundation
1500 Pioneer Building
336 N. Robert Street
St. Paul, MN 55101
(612) 224–1841

Focus: education, arts, and environment.

Award range: $1,000–$17,500.

The McNight Foundation
600 TCF Tower
121 South Eighth Street
Minneapolis, MN 55402
(612) 333–4220

Focus: arts, housing, human and social services.

Award range: $1,500–$2 million.

MISSOURI

Hall Family Foundation
Charitable & Crown Investment 323
P.O. Box 419580
Kansas City, MI 64141
(616) 274–8516

Focus: education, performing and visual arts.

Award range: $20,000–$100,000.

Hallmark Corporate Foundation
P.O. Box 419580
Department 323
Kansas City, MI 64141
(816) 274–8515

Focus: urban affairs, education, social services, arts, youth.

Award range: $200–$10,000.

Yellow Freight System Foundation
10990 Roe Avenue
Overland Park, KS 66207
(913) 345–3000

Focus: civic affairs, cultural programs, social services, education.

Award range: $500–$194,000.

NEW HAMPSHIRE

Norwin S. and Elizabeth N. Bean Foundation
c/o New Hampshire Charitable Fund
One South Street
P.O. Box 1335
Concord, NH 03301
(603) 225–6641

Focus: social and human services, education.

Award range: $2,500–$10,000.

Ellis L. Phillips Foundation
13 Dartmouth College Highway
Lyme, NH 03768
(603) 795–2790

Focus: environment, arts, conservation, social services.

Award range: $1,000–$10,000.

NEW JERSEY

Geraldine R. Dodge Foundation
163 Madison Avenue, 6th Floor
P.O. Box 1239
Morristown, NJ 07962
(201) 540–8442

Focus: environment, energy, animal welfare.

Award range: $15,000–$25,000.

NEW YORK

David and Minnie Berk Foundation
c/o Romm & Berk
1101 Stewart Avenue
Garden City, NY 11530

Focus: social services, Jewish welfare, education, health, and the arts.

Award range: $1,400–$30,000.

Mary Flagler Cary Charitable Trust
350 Fifth Avenue, Room 6622
New York, NY 10018
(212) 563–6860

Focus: environmental, natural resources, and music.

Award range: $10,000–$50,000.

East Hill Foundation
P.O. Box 63
Akron, NY 14001
(716) 759–8620

Focus: performing arts, historic preservation, social services, and community playgrounds.

Award range: $500–$5,000.

Gebbie Foundation, Inc.
Hotel Jamestown Building, Room 308
P.O. Box 1277
Jamestown, NY 14702
(716) 487–1062

Focus: health programs.

Award range: $1,000–$300,000.

A. Lindsay and Olive B. O'Connor Foundation
P.O. Box D
Hobart, NY 13788
(607) 538–9248

Focus: Support for town, village, and environmental improvement.

Award range: $1,000–$20,000.

The Scherman Foundation
315 W. 57th St., Suite 2D
New York, NY 10019
(212) 489–7143

Focus: conservation, human rights, arts, and social services.

Award range: $5,000–$25,000.

The John Ben Snow Foundation
P.O. Box 376
Pulaski, NY 13142
(315) 298–6401
Focus: minority programs, education
Award range: $10,000–$15,000.

The Sulzberger Foundation
229 W. 43rd St.
New York, NY 10036
(212) 556–1750
Focus: education, cultural programs, conservation, and
community service.
Award range: $100–$64,000.

NORTH CAROLINA

Mary Reynolds Babcock Foundation
102 Reynolds Village
Winston-Salem, NC 27106
(919) 748–9222
Focus: social services, community development,
environment.
Award range: $5,000–$35,000.

Kathleen Price and Joseph M. Bryan Family Foundation
One North Pointe, Suite 170
3101 North Elm Street
Greensboro, NC 27408
(919) 288–5455
Focus: education, arts, health, community programs.
Award range: $5,000–$100,000.

James G. Hanes Memorial Fund/Foundation
c/o NCNB National Bank Trust
One NCNB Plaza, TO9-1
Charlotte, NC 28255
(704) 386–8477

Focus: conservation, health, and cultural programs.

Award range: $1,000–$25,000.

OHIO

Community Foundation of Greater Lorain County
1865 North Ridge Road East, Suite A
Lorain, OH 44055
(216) 277–0142

Focus: social services, cultural programs.

Award range: $1,500–$10,000.

Charles H. Dater Foundation
508 Atlas Bank Building
Cincinnati, OH 54202
(513) 241–1234

Focus: social services, fine arts.

Award range: $500–$20,000.

The Reynolds and Reynolds Company Foundation
P.O. Box 2608
Dayton, OH 45401
(513) 449–4490

Focus: local community development, education, health and culture.

Award range: $100–$254,000.

Troy Foundation
c/o Star Bank, NA, Troy
910 West Main St.
Troy, OH 45373
(513) 335–8351

Focus: conservation, cultural programs, recreation, education and community development.

Award range: $500–$195,000.

The Leo Yassenoff Foundation
16 E. Broad Street, Suite 403
Columbus, OH 43215
(614) 221–4315

Focus: social services, education, culture, and minorities.

Award range: $1,000–$20,000.

OREGON

The Collins Foundation
1618 First Avenue, SW, Suite 305
Portland, OR 97201
(503) 227–7171

Focus: art, health, education, cultural programs.

Award range: $5,000–$25,000.

PENNSYLVANIA

Howard Heinz Endowment
30 CNG Tower
625 Liberty Avenue
Pittsburgh, PA 15222
(412) 391–5122

Focus: health, education, and arts.

Award range: $20,000–$500,000.

Lancaster County Foundation
Horst Group Building
29 E. Kind Street, Room 14
Lancaster, PA 17602
(717) 397–1629

Focus: social services, education, and cultural programs.

Award range: $3,000–$10,000.

Richard King Mellon Foundation
One Mellon Bank Center
500 Grant Street, 41st Floor
Pittsburgh, PA 15219
(412) 392–2800

Focus: conservation, social services, wildlife preservation.

Award range: $7,200–$1 million.

The Pittsburgh Foundation
30 CNG Tower
625 Liberty Avenue
Pittsburgh, PA 15222
(412) 391–5122

Focus: urban affairs, education, health, arts.

Award range: $5,000–$70,000.

RHODE ISLAND

Old Stone Bank Charitable Foundation
150 S. Main Street
Providence, RI 02903
(401) 278–2213

Focus: social services, education, and culture

Award range: $1,000–$185,000.

SOUTH CAROLINA

Trident Community Foundation
456 King Street
Charleston, SC 29403
(803) 723–3635

Focus: social services, arts, health, environment, and education.

Award range: $1,500–$5,000.

TEXAS

Communities Foundation of Texas
4605 Live Oak Street
Dallas, TX 75204
(214) 826–5231

Focus: social services, education, health, cultural programs.

Award range: $500–$25,000.

Ken W. Davis Foundation
P.O. Box 3419
Fort Worth, TX 76113
(817) 332–4081

Focus: community development, health, arts.

Award range: $350–$18,700.

El Paso Community Foundation
Texas Commerce Bank Building, Suite 1616
El Paso, TX 79901
(915) 533–4020

Focus: community development, environment, social services, health, education, and arts.

Award range: $500–$25,000.

The Edward and Betty Marcus Foundation
One Preston Center
8222 Douglas, Suite 360
Dallas, TX 75225
(214) 361–4681

Focus: visual arts, education.

Award range: $35,000–$233,000.

Meadows Foundation Inc.
Wilson Historic Block
2922 Swiss Avenue
Dallas, TX 75204
(214) 826–9431

Focus: historic preservation, social services, arts, education, civic concerns.

Award range: $30,000–$60,000.

UTAH

The George S. and Dolores Dore Eccles Foundation
Deseret Building
79 S. Main Street, 12th Floor
Salt Lake City, UT 84111
(801) 350–5336

Focus: education, health, social services, and the arts.

WASHINGTON

Norman Archibald Charitable Foundation
c/o First Interstate Bank of Washington
P.O. Box 21927
Seattle, WA 98111
(206) 292–3543

Focus: conservation, arts, housing, and health.

Award range: $500–$15,000.

Index